A souvenir guide

Sanctuary from the Trenche

Stamford Hospi

C000164311

Sanctuary from the Trenches

To mark the centenary of the beginning of the First World War, this 300-year-old family home has been transformed into a military hospital – The Stamford Hospital – a recreation of the convalescent hospital it became in 1917.

The Saloon before the recreation of the hospital

The Saloon as Bagdad Ward

'I shall never forget the kindness shown to me by yourself, Sister Bennett and all the nurses. Your first thoughts were always for 'the boys' to try and make us as happy and contented as possible.'

An extract taken from Private Carl Montgomery Brodie's letter to Lady Stamford, December 1917

Almost 300 soldiers were cared for here between 1917 and 1919. They were low-ranking servicemen, their backgrounds often at odds with the privileged surroundings they found themselves in. Yet the Grey family whose home it was – led by the redoubtable Lady Stamford – made these men wonderfully welcome. The quiet country house and its idyllic gardens became the backdrop not solely for medical care but for boating, croquet, cricket and squash which were laid on for men whose injuries were often as much psychological as they were physical.

The two-year transformation of Dunham Massey today is a remarkable one, just as it was then, 100 years ago. Gone are the elegant Edwardian interiors. In place of the Saloon is a 14-bed hospital ward. The Great Hall is once again the soldiers' recreation room. The Billiard Room is the nurses' station, while the foot of the Grand Staircase is the operating theatre that the young Lady Jane Grey remembers so vividly.

The First World War wasn't, as it was hoped, the war to end all wars. It disrupted life for millions of ordinary people across the world – there was no hiding from its savagery. We commemorate this First World War by marking one family's attempt to face up to the bloodiest conflict in British military history, by providing its battered soldiers with the comforts of the Stamford Hospital, a sanctuary from the trenches.

Above Elizabeth Louisa Penelope Grey, Countess of Stamford and her two children, Roger Grey, later 10th Earl of Stamford and Lady Jane Grey, later Lady Turnbull, by John Ernest Breun, 1904

'It was more like lifting the screen of war from a beautiful old house that seemed to breathe peace from its walls. It had borne with a grace and dignity the demands that war had made upon it.'

A nurse's note written in the Stamford Hospital Book about the day Armistice was declared, November 1918

Turning a House into a Hospital

Few expected the war to last. Many believed it would be over by Christmas. But as the troops dug in and the number of dead and injured continued to rise, the conflict drained the country's existing resources. It became apparent that if Britain was to going to win the war, additional help was needed, and much of that help needed to be medical. In response, the British Red Cross and the Order of St John formed the Joint War Committee; together they supplied all manner of services, from transport to the training of the volunteer (or 'VAD') nurses who would become so vital to the war effort.

Below New patients on stretchers arriving at the front of the house

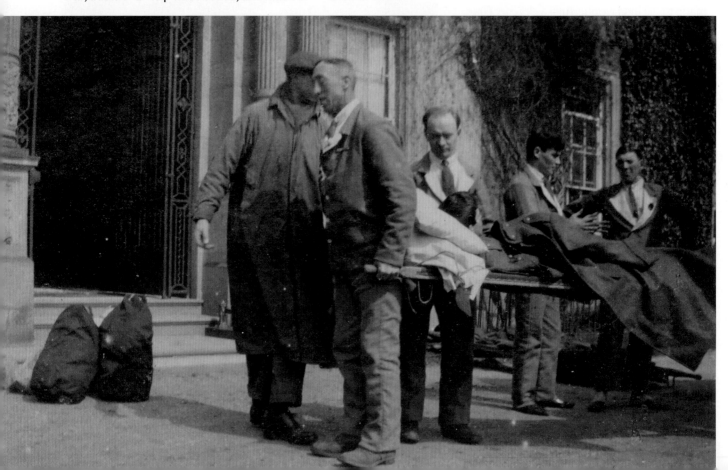

Overwhelmed services

Many of the facilities we now take for granted didn't exist during the First World War. What hospitals Britain had were quickly overwhelmed, forcing the Joint War Committee to look elsewhere for support. Dunham Massey was just such a house. Located three miles from Altrincham's hospital (and not far from Manchester should specialist care be needed), its size combined with the fact that it was occupied by only three people and their staff – Roger Grey, the 10th Earl of Stamford, his mother Penelope, the Countess of Stamford and his sister, Lady Jane, made it ideal. Roger and Lady Stamford offered up their home willingly, and when it opened in 1917, it became one of almost 3,300 auxiliary hospitals across the country.

Above The Quartermaster, Mr Perkins, entering names in the admission book

Right The hospital rules

Stamford Hospital

MEALS.

Breakfast	-	-	7-45	a.m.
Dinner	-	-	12-15	p.m.
Tea	-	-	5-0	p.m.
Supper	-	-	8-15	p.m.

Patients are asked not to smoke in the Ward before 8 a.m. or after 9 p.m., or while the **Doctor** is in the Ward. They are requested to use an Ash Tray always when smoking.

Patients are asked to help with the work of the Hospital, as directed by the **Matron.**

Patients can be out after 10 a.m. They will not be absent from Meals without permission from the **Matron** or **Sister in Charge.** Passes issued at 10 a.m. by the **Matron.** Patients can have One Pass during the week, and one, in addition, on Sundays.

Patients must be in the Hospital by   p.m. Patients who wish to remain to **Tea** must ask permission before 1 p.m.

A **Bell** will be rung at   p.m. for Roll Call.

Certain parts of the Grounds are marked **"Private"** or **"Out of Bounds."** Patients are asked to respect these notice boards.

Patients are forbidden to take **Visitors** in the Boat.

Prayers	-	-	8-45	p.m.
Ward	-	-	9-0	p.m.
Lights Out	-	-	9-30	p.m.

Visiting Days:
Sundays and Wednesdays, 2 p.m. to 4 p.m.

Background to the Hospital: Trench Warfare

The First World War was one of the most deadly in world history, killing an estimated nine million people and resulting in death, destruction, injury and disease on an unprecedented scale. It was a war marked by a clash of two military styles: of armies bolstered by technological advances yet hampered by tactics that had failed to keep pace. So while armies still relied on men on foot to attack the enemy, those soldiers were now met by the sorts of weapons – machine guns, poison gas, field artillery – capable of inflicting lethal damage swiftly and from a distance. The result was utter carnage. 'Digging in' offered the only form of protection from the onslaught. Trench warfare was born and with it went any hope of a quick and decisive end to the war.

The chain of evacuation

The route from the Front to a hospital was a complex one. A soldier followed a system of treatment that started in the trenches and ended – if he was lucky – on British soil. It began with the stretcher bearers, who pulled the injured out of no-man's-land and gave basic first aid. Next came the Regional Aid Post, close to the front line and where additional first aid was given. About 400 yards further back was the Advanced Dressing Station. Better supplied, stocked with morphine, anti-tetanus serum and treatments for the gassed, it was nevertheless so close to the Front that it could only hope to patch up the injured.

Those unable to walk were taken to the Main Dressing Station about a mile away, facilities that were equipped with surgical instruments for use in an emergency. The more seriously injured went on to the Casualty Clearing Station, usually located around eight or nine miles from the front line. Here, for the first time, was a reasonably staffed medical team: surgeons, for example, trained military nurses and equipment such as X-ray machines.

If a soldier had survived thus far, his next port of call was a General Hospital (Stationary Hospital). Positioned well behind the lines, these requisitioned buildings boasted facilities such as radiography and specialists such as bacteriologists, and it was from here that those deemed well enough to travel were evacuated back to England. They were tended by experienced nursing staff who changed dressings and focused on preventing infection – apparently taking instructions from a card, written by the hospital medical staff and then hung around a soldier's neck. Once back in England, soldiers were usually allocated to an auxiliary hospital – and for 282 soldiers serving during the First World War, that hospital was here at Dunham Massey.

Opposite left The 'Strand' War Map of Central Europe showing European frontiers, 1914, with small paper flags attached to metal pins stuck through the map in various places

Opposite right *An Advanced Dressing Station*, by Henry Tonks 1918

Below A Casualty Clearing Station. 'Tenderly lifting a serious case.' Stretcher bearers at work, 1915

Life in the trenches

By the end of 1914, the trenches that ran along the Western Front stretched for 475 miles, from the North Sea and Belgium, through France to the Swiss border. Here, men hunkered down in parallel trenches that had been scratched out of the soil, with a desolate 'no-man's-land' between. There are no words that can adequately describe the horror of the conditions those men faced. Of mud so thick that a man taking shelter in a shell crater might get stuck and drown. Of the overwhelming stench of rotting flesh, of rats the size of dogs, of the deafening noise and smell of artillery fire and mustard gas.

The constant mud, damp and often freezing conditions, along with rats and lice, spread diseases – some of which had never been seen before. By the end of 1914, for example, 20,000 British troops had suffered from the previously unknown 'trench foot'; amputation often followed. As supplies dwindled, hunger was rife, the soldiers grubbing around for what food they could find. Survival on the Front wasn't limited to avoiding the constant threat of German gunfire. The enemy here was also hunger, fatigue, incessant damp, disease and biting cold – and the men who arrived at the Stamford Hospital were not just injured. They were often filthy, malnourished and traumatised.

The Main Figures behind the Hospital

The First World War may have been played out in distant battlefields, but its effects were nevertheless felt close to home. Ordinary houses were, as we shall see, turned into hospitals. Zeppelins appeared in the southern skies, while the absence of young men, particularly those 'pals' from small communities who joined up together, was marked. Many women volunteered as nurses. Others abandoned domestic service in favour of the new jobs now open to them; some two million replaced men in factories and other places of work.

Dunham Massey witnessed these changes on a smaller scale. The young men who worked in the house, garden and estate joined up. And while from 1917 the household was led by the young Roger Grey, 10th Earl of Stamford, the house itself was most likely offered up to the military by his mother, Penelope – with the running of the Stamford Hospital falling almost entirely to her. It was a huge responsibility and a mammoth administrative effort. Yet, as we shall see, it was a task she ably took on.

The main figures behind the hospital

Penelope Grey, Countess of Stamford, a widow who single-handedly ran the Dunham Massey estate from 1910 until her son Roger came of age

Lady Jane Grey, just 15 when war broke out, Roger's younger sister spent much of the war serving as a volunteer nurse

Sister Catherine Bennett, the matron who led the nursing team at the hospital; a tireless and dedicated nurse

Roger Grey, the 10th Earl of Stamford, who inherited the house and estate in 1917, but who spent much of the war on duty in London

Opposite Sister Bennett, Dr Harry Gordon Cooper and Nurse Perkins dressed for surgery

'Mother's name appears in *The Times* today among a list of people mentioned for valuable services rendered in connection with the convalescent hospitals.'

Roger Grey's diary entry, 9 April 1919

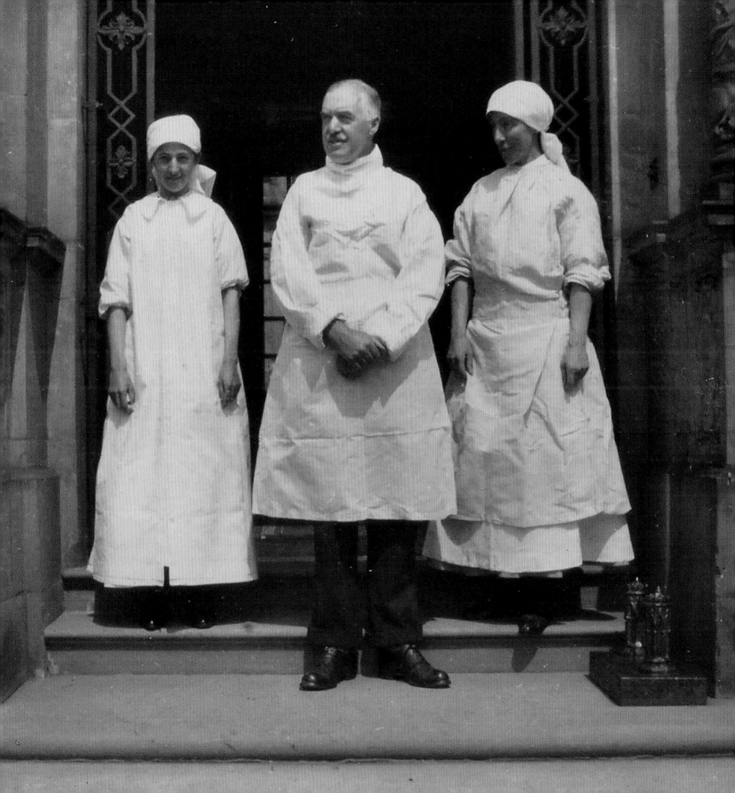

Penelope Grey, Countess of Stamford, Commandant

Penelope Grey, Countess of Stamford, had proven herself a capable woman well before the onset of war. Her husband had died unexpectedly in 1910, leaving her in sole charge of two young children and an estate that was only partway through an extensive restoration. Yet she picked up the reins and took over the management of house and estate to the extent that she felt able to convert her home into a hospital and then become its 'commandant' when it opened in 1917. In many ways, it made sense. Lady Stamford was the Vice President of the Altrincham division of the British Red Cross, and, like many aristocrats of the period, was fiercely patriotic. Organised and possessed of a strategic mind, she was able to oversee the administrative running of the hospital with apparent ease.

She was also a formidable woman who guarded the family's place in society at a time when class boundaries were beginning to be worn away. Even in the 1930s, for example, she expected boys living on the estate to doff their caps when she passed by. Yet despite this reputation – and her social standing – Lady Stamford's interest in the hospital remained with her patients. She spent time with the first batches of soldiers admitted to Altrincham General Hospital and when away from Dunham would often write to her daughter, asking Jane to keep an eye on a particular soldier she was worried about. It was an interest that was reciprocated and there are many letters from former soldiers and their families, written to Lady Stamford to thank her for her care.

Left Lady Jane Grey

Lady Jane Grey, VAD Nurse

Lady Jane Grey, the Earl of Stamford's younger sister, greeted news of the outbreak of war like so many of her peers, with a curious sense of elation. 'I was in the bathroom upstairs, and my brother shouted through the door in great excitement … we've declared war on Germany, war's broken out! It was the spirit of the time that everybody was thrilled,' she remembered years later.

It was a sentiment that wasn't to last. At just 16, she began helping at a nearby convalescent hospital, Haigh Lawn in Altrincham, and in 1917, like many upper and middle class girls of her generation, volunteered as a VAD (Voluntary Aid Detachment) nurse. Hers was a basic training, one that focused on cleaning, hygiene and first aid (or acting 'like a parlour maid'). But alongside these basic duties, VAD nurses such as Jane provided another service. As the war dragged on, fully trained nurses found themselves increasingly stretched and it was often the VAD nurses who filled in the gaps, providing comfort for patients suffering from profound psychological trauma, or for men with life-changing injuries. It was a level of care that was gratefully received – as evidenced by Jane's scrapbook, which she kept from her time at Haigh Lawn. In it, Sapper Nearney of the Royal Engineers, wounded in a mine explosion in July 1916, composed a tribute to the young nurse: 'It is in her to soothe sorrow and pain away, and with her smile equip a soldier once more for the fray. It's worthwhile fighting for such as Nurse Grey.'

At the Stamford Hospital, Lady Jane proved herself equally capable. She was promoted to a more senior role, one that saw her changing dressings and assisting at an operation. 'My word, what those poor men suffered,' she said of her medical experiences and by the time the hospital closed, Jane felt very differently about the war from the young girl who saw it in.

'I have never had a keener nurse than Lady Jane. I try to keep her back, but it's no use. I do not think it is doing her any harm, on the contrary she is decidedly happier and will do anything to get me off duty in the P.M. so that she can stay on and [write] the report.'

An extract taken from Sister Catherine Bennett's letter to Roger Grey, 25 September 1917

Below A tambourine signed by patients and given to Nurse Grey on her 18th birthday

'This morning eight cot cases arrived, six surgical and two medical. Several have only been in England a few days. They are all dead tired and seem to need sleep badly. They are all marked severe on the case-sheets but I think a week here will make a big improvement.'

Sister Catherine Bennett writing to Roger Grey, 4 April 1918

Opposite Mr Perkins, Quartermaster, and Sister Bennett in the garden

Right Sister Catherine Bennett

Right below Sister Bennett dressing Sergeant Percy Chaplin's leg outside

Sister Catherine Bennett

For almost all of its operation, Stamford Hospital was run by Sister Catherine Bennett, its matron. Dedicated to what she saw as 'her' hospital, she worked at Dunham Massey until the last patient left in 1919, and often put the care of her patients above everything else. In one case, she urged that a soldier she suspected of developing an aneurysm be allowed to stay in her one-to-one care, rather than take the life-threatening journey to a more fully equipped hospital. Dr Cooper agreed, and the man survived. In another, she put her relationship with the Grey family on the line by writing to Roger to protest against Lady Stamford's decision to temporarily close two wards in 1918. This decision had been taken in order to relieve the desperately overworked staff, including Sister Bennett, who were running the hospital. This was one argument she lost; the hospital closed for six weeks in 1918, though it didn't appear to damage the relationship between Sister Bennett and the woman she fondly called 'my commandant'.

After the war, Sister Bennett kept in touch with the family, writing to Lady Stamford from the Serbian Relief Fund Hospital in the Balkans where she went to in late 1919. Ever the professional, she'd been asked to take charge of an isolation ward with typhus cases which she described as 'very thrilling'. She never forgot her time at the Stamford Hospital: she also wrote that she remembered Lady Stamford as one who had taught her so much and was just like a mother to her.

Roger Grey, 10th Earl of Stamford

Roger Grey, 10th Earl of Stamford, was 17 when the First World War broke out and, although he officially took over management of the house and estate when he came of age in October 1917, it was in fact Lady Stamford who ran the hospital. The reason why is simple: Roger spent most of his war in London, serving as an aide-de-camp to Lieutenant General Sir Francis Lloyd, the man responsible for the defence of the capital and who rose during the war to become the General Officer Commanding London District. It was a position that kept Roger so busy it allowed him to pay only occasional visits home. Yet he still played an essential part in the running of the hospital. He used his position in London to acquire medical supplies and equipment and, via regular correspondence, developed a close and supportive relationship with its matron, Sister Bennett.

Roger Grey in uniform

Like his mother, Roger took a keen personal interest in patient welfare; on his first visit in August 1917 he toured the ward and shook hands with every soldier, while on his coming of age, the staff and 18 of its patients, led by Sergeant Percy Chaplin, sent him a letter of congratulation, wishing him every success and promising a 'little token of respect' by separate post. Private Greenhalgh went further and composed a lengthy poem. It is thanks to Roger Grey's meticulously kept records that we are able to glean so much essential information about the hospital that would otherwise have been lost.

Below A group of soldiers and nurses in the garden. Back row, left to right: Whitehead, Ball, Pirie, McDonald, Bownes; Second row from back, left to right: Ditchburn, Topham, Brodie, Smith, Nurse Meriel, Beattie, Edwards, Smith; Second row from front, left to right: Osborne, Mrs Bullock, Matron, Nurse Wyatt, Sanderson; Front row, left to right: Greenhalgh, Nurse Shirley, Burgess

The medical hierarchy at Stamford Hospital

Although run by the British Red Cross, Stamford was a military institution and was organised accordingly. Its hierarchical structure, designed to provide a familiar, barracks-like environment for the soldiers, was set out in the 1918 British Red Cross Handbook, and comprised:

The Commandant, Lady Stamford: who took overall responsibility for the management and running of the hospital.

The Medical Officers: Drs Percy Robert and Harry Gordon Cooper, fully trained doctors who were likely to have worked across several auxiliary hospitals in the area

A Quarter Master: Mrs Bullock and then Mr Perkins. Responsible for receipt and management of supplies, medical and otherwise, for the hospital

The Matron: Sister Catherine Bennett who reported to the Commandant

Nurses, including Lady Jane Grey: a mix of professional nurses and trained volunteers

Dr Harry Gordon Cooper

'My word what those
wretched men suffered'
A quote from Lady Jane in an
oral history interview, 1986

Gassed, by John Singer Sargent, 1919

Hard Work and Good Nursing

'Glad to hear about Dunham being turned into a hospital.
A very good thing …'

An extract taken from Lady Jane Grey's
letter to her mother, February 1917

The Stamford Hospital was a modest affair, opening in April 1917 with just 25 beds contained within a single ward. Sixteen patients were admitted on its first day, suffering from a mixture of conditions – from bullet and shrapnel wounds to influenza – that would become typical for the hospital's admissions. It's very first patient was Rifleman Thomas Hibbits of the 1st Battalion Royal Irish Rifles; he was recovering from the (now virtually extinct) condition of trench foot and would be discharged back to duty two months later.

It may have been called a hospital – and run extremely efficiently – but Stamford Hospital was far removed from today's expectations of healthcare. Often, staff worked in less than ideal conditions. Lady Jane remembers the operating theatre, which, situated at the foot of the Grand Staircase, was 'extremely unhygienic. I mean, cobwebs could have fallen down there!' The work was hard and often done by hand. Jane remembers washing the 'awful bandages' in the bathroom, while Sister Bennett, despite being terribly shorthanded at times, undertook bed baths herself 'as it's too hard for the nurses to do properly' – this on top of giving surgical patients a 'Lysol (disinfectant) bath' and disinfecting the bath after each patient. With the doctors visiting only infrequently, this hard work fell almost solely to the nurses, and they were expected to turn their hand to anything.

Below A Service badge

ALTRINCHAM WAR HOSPITAL SUPPLY DEPÔT,
SERVICE BADGE.

'The Saloon as a ward is a charming place.'
An extract taken from Roger Grey's diary,
30 August 1917

The daily routine: nurses

The daily routine was regimented and regular – for both staff and patients. For VAD nurses, each 12-hour shift began with a uniform inspection (spotlessly clean, no ankles on show); matron would also keep an eye on nurses' interactions with patients (no over familiarity). The VADs would then be allocated tasks, which ranged from making beds, cooking, and reading to those patients unable to do so themselves, to changing dressings, emptying bed pans and giving bed baths.

Medical complaints

Over the course of its short life, the Stamford Hospital treated conditions ranging from bullet wounds to shell shock, illness caused by being gassed, broken limbs and fractures, influenza, pneumonia, nephritis, trench fever and trench foot. Complications from seemingly simple injuries could often at the Front become life threatening, and many of the treatments we take for granted today – such as the use of blood transfusions – were still in their infancy then. The real skill was thus in giving individual care; adapting what treatments and facilities were available to meet the needs of the vastly different and almost always psychologically traumatised patients.

The daily routine: patients

7.45 am – breakfast followed by medicine rounds, cleaning, changing dressings, administering treatment

10 am – passes issued by Matron – (to leave the ward; one per week plus another on Sundays)

12.15 pm – dinner followed by medicine rounds, massage and exercise, and letter writing

5 pm – tea followed by the final medicine round of the day

8.15 pm – supper

8.45 pm – prayers

9 pm – ward round

9.30 pm – lights out

Visiting – Sundays and Wednesdays only, 2–4 pm

Risk of infection

In a time when we have access to antibiotics, it is hard to imagine just how lethal infections could be. In 1917 even a minor injury could prove fatal, and thus one of the most pressing concerns for the nurses at Dunham was the control, prevention or eradication of infection. And it was why Sister Bennett often changed the dressings herself – the risk to her patients if a volunteer nurse got it wrong were just too great. One of Sister Bennett's main tasks was thus to help her nurses understand the importance of sterilisation and disinfection.

Everything was in short supply and, as supplies ran low, more basic treatments had to be used. Sphagnum moss was one. This bog-moss had been used as a wound dressing for millennia, its absorbent properties performing better than the cotton wool it replaced. It was sanctioned by the War Office as an acceptable dressing and, by the end of the war, over a million pads a month were being produced in Britain. Elsewhere, nurses became adept at recognising and treating the different kinds of toxins that frontline soldiers had been gassed with.

Fresh air cure

Sister Bennett also encouraged post-operative patients to spend time in the gardens. Dr Cooper admitted to being very interested in Sister Bennett's 'fresh air cure', which seemed to consist of patients spending as much time as possible out of doors and even being stationed in a shed in the grounds. One such patient was Private Fred Lomas, 1st Battalion Lincolnshire Regiment, who, despite suffering from tuberculosis, recovered enough within three months of being admitted to Stamford Hospital to be discharged to light duties. Whatever the medical benefits of Sister Bennett's approach, it is likely that being outside provided a boost to recovering soldiers. 'The men love the gardens, you should see our dressing gown parade,' she told Roger Grey in a letter in May 1918.

> 'Patient's leg was in a very septic condition on admission and recovery was doubtful.'
>
> Sister Bennett's comments
> about Private Hadley

> 'Patient's chief trouble was 'nerves' the result of shell shock.'
>
> Sister Bennett's comments
> about Rifleman Allison

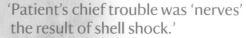

Shell shock and trauma

It wasn't all sunny days spent in the garden. In a letter to her brother, Jane mentions a pleasant day with the men out on the lake when suddenly one went 'off his head and said and did fearful things'. Sister Bennett, meanwhile, noted in 1918 that of a 'little convoy' of 12 new patients, only two were able to walk and all were depressed, 'mainly due, I think, to their physical condition' – one had been gassed, almost blinded and wounded in the leg. 'He is a pitiable object and is so grateful for the slightest thing, and says he didn't know such kindness existed.'

Left The Moss Garden at Dunham Massey today

Below: 'Fresh air treatment'

What was the Carrel-Dakin treatment?

Painful, cold and unpleasant, this was a treatment worth enduring. It often had a dramatic impact on wounds that may otherwise have proven fatal. Henry Dakin and Alexis Carrel were chemists who, in response to the war, developed a new system of wound-cleaning that revolutionised the treatment of injured soldiers, irrigating the wound with a highly diluted antiseptic made from sodium hypochlorite and boric acid. Rubber tubes were packed deep into the wound and bandaged into place, delivering a constant flow of the solution to the injury. The tubes were removed every two to three days, sterilised, cultures taken and, if the infection had abated, the wound would be stitched up.

'I have started the 'sun cure' for wounds …'
An extract taken from Sister Bennett's letter to Roger Grey, 8 May 1918

The Hospital Suit.

Here's to the suit of light grey and blue
    Which the richest on earth may not buy!
And here's to the cap of a nondescript hue!
    And here's to the <u>loose</u> red tie

The jacket's not cut on the smartest of lines
    And the trousers may bag at the knees
While the shoes perhaps, shew unmistakable signs
    That there fashioned entirely for ease.

But the Real'est Real, as he strolls down the Mall
    With the latest in spats, and in ties,
Cannot vie with T. Atkins, when out with a pall
    In the suit which <u>his</u> country supplies.

In these fashions for men there is little that's new,
    But the one which is worn with most pride,
Is surely the jacket with one sleeve in view,
    And the other pinned down to the side

Fellow Brittons, whom age or misfortune debars
    From a share in your country's release,
Who never can earn by the right of your scars
    The Thanks of <u>a nation</u> at Peace.

Does the sight of these lads, (there are thousands about
call to mind that they've suffered for you.

Then your hats well come off.
and your hearts wring you out.
To the boys in the light grey & Blue

a game of Cards.

A. Croque

Tou

urnament. July 1918

the ...al.

UNION JACK CLUB,

31, STAMFORD STREET,
ALTRINCHAM
- (NEXT TO THE HIPPODROME). -

The Patients of this Hospital are invited to make use of the above Club;

Open daily from **2-30 p.m.** to **9 p.m.**
Sundays   -   **2-30** „ „ **5** „

The Club contains a

**READING ROOM,   GAMES ROOM,
CANTEEN,   BILLIARD ROOM.**

Concerts and Entertainments are frequently given.

All Soldiers in Uniform will be welcome. They are invited to bring their girl friends with them.

C. E. R. ABBOTT,
Hon. Sec.

'The Most Perfectly Beautiful Hospital in the Land'

A quote from an article in *The Queen, The Lady's Newspaper*, 8 November 1918

It is clear from countless records, letters and documents that for the soldiers who passed through Dunham Massey during the First World War, it was more than simply a medical institution. A sense of almost maternal care underpinned the Stamford Hospital – and it began with the close ties between Lady Stamford, her children and Sister Bennett. They were all fond of each other, the relationship between Jane and her mother being exceptionally close, and that between

Sister Bennett and the family likewise. Sister Bennett writes frequently and without formality to Roger, for example, saying of the Countess in one letter, 'she is so good to me, I wish I could do twice as much for her'.

Despite everything – the family's aristocratic status, the soldiers' experiences, the military environment – what comes across from surviving records is a pervading sense of care and respect. And not just between the family and their staff, but between them and

'There was another whist drive at 6 in which I played. Mother gave away the prizes and got the booby prize herself.'

An extract taken from Roger Grey's diary, 7 March 1918

Left **The recreation room in the Great Hall**

Opposite **The Great Hall**

the soldiers. Lady Stamford would, for example, ask others to look out for particular patients while she was away. 'I wonder why you mention Smith [a patient] as specifically needing a kind word,' writes Jane to her mother in August 1917. 'He is the brightest and gayest of the lot and is always very nice in helping me at the meals.' Jane similarly became attached, while Sister Bennett wrote of one severely injured soldier, 'I feel I cannot do enough for him'. There are moving letters from the time which tell of the strong connection many of the soldiers made with Dunham … and from the grateful mothers who were thankful for the time their sons spent in the care of the Stamford Hospital.

Recreation and entertainment

Dunham could not have been further from the soldiers' experiences of the trenches. With the hospital opening in 1917, many of those who came to the Stamford Hospital knew that they would go back to the Front. The easy, privileged life of Dunham Massey was one that few patients had experienced – they were ordinary rank and file soldiers, not officers. Yet the family was keen to give the men the chance to enjoy themselves.

The Great Hall became their recreation room, where they played the piano, games or listened to music. A gramophone was in use on Sister Bennett's ward where the worst surgical cases were put, so that she could attend to them herself. Nurse Joan Shirley played the violin (she also helped Private Harvey of the 2nd Hampshire Regiment get over his shell-shock-induced stammer by giving him lessons and exercises).

The less seriously wounded went boating on the moat; a few fishermen were out on the water as early as 6.45am, according to Jane. She noted in a letter in 1917 that the weather 'has been so warm, that I am writing this in the garden. The punt is on the moat, and the soldiers are on the water all day'. The men also played cricket, tennis and squash. There are invoices in the household records that note the purchase of croquet sets and port for the soldiers. There were talks from Canon Wainwright on a Friday after tea, lectures, films and whist drives, and occasional trips out, such as to the theatre in Manchester.

'In the evening the men gave a concert …'
An extract taken from Roger Grey's diary, 4 September 1917

Real People, Real Lives

The Stamford Hospital treated 282 men but 100 years later trying to find out who they were was not easy.

What is known however, is that some of them kept in touch with the family after their discharge. A few stand out, the letters and photographs they left behind giving an insight into their lives and, occasionally, answering one of the most urgent questions surrounding their treatment – did they survive the war?

Right A Christmas card sent from Carl Brodie to Lady Stamford

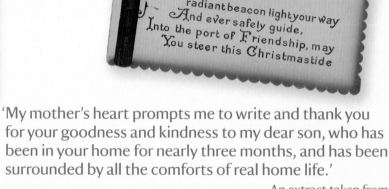

GUNNER
CARL MONTGOMERGY
BRODIE

Admission number: 30
Admitted: 26 June 1917
Discharged:
   25 September 1917
Eventually returned to active duty

Carl Brodie wrote frequently to Lady Stamford, writing in January 1918, to thank her for a Christmas present of writing paper and pencils; he was also one of 11 patients who wrote to Roger Grey to congratulate him on his coming of age in 1917. It wasn't, however, only the young private who wrote to Lady Stamford. His mother did too, to thank her for looking after her beloved son. Carl had several correspondences with Lady Stamford who invited him for Christmas 1917, but he had to 'stay put' as he was due to be posted back to France at any time. 'I must say I was not struck with the idea of coming out again,' he wrote

'My mother's heart prompts me to write and thank you for your goodness and kindness to my dear son, who has been in your home for nearly three months, and has been surrounded by all the comforts of real home life.'

An extract taken from
Margaret Montgomery Brodie's letter to Lady Stamford, October 1917

in April 1918, 'but now that I am into it, I do not mind it so much. It's funny the way a person gets used to this life again even though it has many hardships.' The three stayed in contact until the end of the war, and it is through their letters that we know Carl survived his second posting to the Front – despite contracting 'flu' there.

PRIVATE
WILLIAM FINDLAY,
HIGHLAND LIGHT
INFANTRY 12TH

Admission number: 42
Admitted: 13 August 1917
Discharged: 27 March 1918
to command depot

William Findlay was admitted to the Stamford Hospital with ten shrapnel wounds in the arm, leg and thigh, and faced three operations at the hospital. Following his discharge from Dunham to St George's Hospital in Stockport, he wrote to Lady Stamford to thank her for the kindness she showed to his mother and sister when they came to visit him at Dunham. Through his letter we know that Mrs Findlay and her daughter arrived at Dunham in the rain, and Lady Stamford went outside to meet them. Having travelled from Scotland to see William, the women had no place to stay and Lady Stamford organised accommodation in the village.

Mrs Findlay wrote to Lady Stamford following her visit, 'I thank God that he was not killed like his dear Brother however there's nothing but sad homes this new year … I'm glad to hear he's looking better that when I seen [sic] him and I know that when his leg is healed he will be very sorry to come home and leave you all'.

Below A group photo showing Private William Findlay (front row, right)

PRIVATE
JOHN WILLIAM
(JACK) DITCHBURN,
9TH YORKS

Admission number: 36
Admitted: 30 June 1917
Discharged: 3 September
    1917 to active duty

PRIVATE
EDWIN MOXON,
KING'S OWN YORKSHIRE
LIGHT INFANTRY

Admission number: 8
Admitted: 24 April 1917
Discharged: 29 June 1917
    to active duty

Edwin Moxon, a Yorkshireman from Pontefract, wrote in August 1917 to ask Lady Stamford if she could send a copy of the photograph of her, the nurses, the patients and the doctor, taken before he was discharged. She sent it off immediately and he replied with news as to what had happened after he left Dunham Massey. Unable to lift heavy weights due to his previous arm injury, he was deemed unfit for the infantry. He was transferred to the Machine Gun Corps, not a particularly suitable new role, given the need to lift and move heavy guns! He hoped for 'a speedy termination of hostilities to the betterment and good of civilisation'.

John Ditchburn was another soldier whose mother felt moved to write to Lady Stamford. Mrs Ditchburn thanked her in September 1917 for the care given to her son, and asked Lady Stamford not to tell her son that she'd written. She wrote once more, the following February, and it was this letter that gave some clue as to the hardships faced by the families of many of the soldiers who went to war. By then, Mrs Ditchburn wrote that her son was back in hospital with a septic foot injury, her eldest daughter had lost her job, their rented house had been condemned which forced them to move somewhere more expensive (the rent being more money than her husband brought home). 'I hope you will not be vexed at this letter,' she said, 'as I wanted to tell someone, and then I can pull myself together. If you had seen the letters he [John Ditchburn] wrote home from your house, you would have been rewarded for your love and care.' There was perhaps a happier ending in sight: John received a medal, survived the war and died in Huddersfield in 1978.

SERGEANT WALTER
G. HAMMOND, 24TH
ROYAL FUSILIERS

Admission number: 279
Admitted: 15 December
    1918
Discharge date: not known
Discharged fit

Walter Hammond wrote a letter to Lady Stamford in January 1922 in which he recalled Christmas at Dunham, the memory being triggered by seeing a dog similar to Buzz, the Grey family's dog:

Your Ladyship will, I hope, both understand and forgive the impulse which prompts an old patient of Stamford Hall to write to you. We Tommies, I am afraid, took one hardship or other as a matter of course, while 'grousing' impartially at both; it is only when Time gets things into the right perspective that we realise that the outstanding features of our convalescence were the sympathy and self-denial of the great-hearted men and women with whom we came in contact. It was the entrance of a dog like Buzz at a Christmas party last week that set me reminiscing. I saw the old fellow chasing a draught along the hall floor, and suddenly stop and turn away disconsolately as it took sanctuary in the ward. Then the Christmas tree, the heavily laden table, the huge Yule-log fire, and the happy fraternity of staff and patients came back in a flash and my first New Year's resolution was formed. As one of the many who were fortunate enough to experience the pleasure of your generous hospitality, may I offer your Ladyship my humble but heartfelt thanks.

Expansion, Pressure and Closure

Although Stamford Hospital opened relatively late in the war, it nevertheless struggled with the increasing numbers of patients. Documents reveal that the housekeeper, Mrs Collins, helped turn Lady Stamford's Sitting Room into an isolation ward. Housemaid Mabel Doody, meanwhile, was seconded to the hospital for a few hours each day, though for her that extra work had a happy outcome: it was on the ward that she met Sergeant Percy Chaplin, the soldier who later became her husband.

By early 1918, the hospital began taking on more severely injured patients, something Sister Bennett had anticipated when she converted the space at the foot of the Grand Staircase into a simple operating theatre. Soon, operations were being scheduled here regularly, while more rooms were opened up:

a small ward of 12 beds placed in the Chintz Drawing Room, an isolation ward created in Lady Stamford's Parlour and a specialist eye ward set up to help those soldiers whose sight had been damaged by gas. But the patients kept on coming. One of the most astounding procedures involved the removal of shrapnel from a soldier's brain. The young Jane Grey assisted, later describing her task – holding a torch as a surgeon performed a trepan – simply as 'a job that had to be done'. Although the patient, Private Johnstone, seemed at first to have come out of surgery well – he was sitting up in bed and asking for a cup of tea only an hour later – he died shortly afterwards following his transfer to Manchester Royal Infirmary for more specialist care.

Above A recreation of the operating theatre at the foot of the Grand Staircase

Below 1917. Standing at back, left to right: Wragg, Peacock, Burns with Buzz the dog, Warrell, Laskey; front, left to right: Timms, Wee Jock, Hodson

Sergeant Percy Chaplin

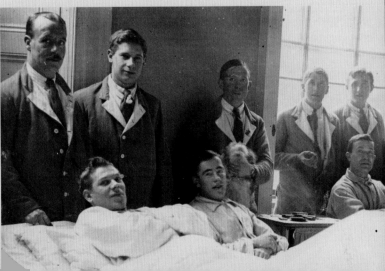

'Mabel is a splendid help, and she loves it, I think it's done the servants good just lately, to see how hard we really all work in the hospital.'

An extract taken from Sister Bennett's letter to Roger Grey, April 1918

Behind the Scenes

'I am discharging the men as quickly as possible now, beds are wanted badly.'

An extract taken from Sister Bennett's letter to Roger Grey, 23 April 1918

In April 1918, the hospital had expanded once more. There were so many patients that Sister Bennett had to arrange a rota, running from 6am–9.20pm every day, just to get through the soldiers' baths. She was constantly on call, while new arrivals appeared to be coming in fresh from the Front, often with complex injuries. Of the six patients admitted on 22 April, one was 'gassed and almost blind, two had leg wounds, one had five shrapnel wounds, injuries to his hands and face, and a tube in his abdomen. One young man had uncleaned wounds in both legs and one arm … poor little chap looks so ill, am afraid he has some virulent germs,' Sister Bennett reported to Roger Grey.

But while Sister Bennett was determined to manage no matter how tough things got, Lady Stamford was not. Recognising the strain the matron – and the hospital as a whole – was under, she told Sister Bennett one morning in July 1918 that she thought the hospital should reduce its capacity. It didn't go down well; Sister Bennett immediately wrote to Roger to make a case for keeping all of its wards open. It was a risky move, asking a son to go against his mother's wishes, but both Roger and Lady Stamford understood how difficult it was for Sister Bennett to take a step back.

Lady Stamford knew, too, that Sister Bennett would never admit to being overworked and so, instead of asking her to take leave, she merely asked her to reduce the number of beds. What happened next we can't be sure, but by the beginning of August, Sister Bennett had changed her mind – and so had Lady Stamford, who decided instead to close the hospital completely for six weeks.

'Of course being quite full it made things very hard, but everybody has been so good really there has been no hardship about it, except that I wish I was stronger and never got tired.'

An extract taken from Sister Bennett's letter to Roger Grey, April 1918

'I said no, it would not be the right thing to do. Lord Stamford, can't you tell me the reason for all this, why [I] cannot go on as I have done? I don't feel that I can alter my decision, namely I shall not send in a return of less than 56 equipped beds.'

An extract taken from Sister Bennett's letter to Roger Grey, 27 July 1918

Above Soldiers on the ward steps after dinner, July 1917

August 1918 saw the start of a new allied strategy, the Hundred Days Offensive, designed to weaken the German defences which eventually brought the war to a close, but causing an increase in casualties. When the Stamford Hospital opened again on 1 October, 27 patients were admitted on its first day, one whose leg was only saved from amputation by constant changes of dressings.

'Well Boys, Perhaps it's Peace'

'If only you could have been here on Monday. At first they could not take the good news in, then followed a glorious pillow fight!! They went quite mad. I fetched Mrs. Collins and they pelted her, we all lost our caps.'

An extract taken from Sister Bennett's letter to Roger Grey, 14 November 1918

One nurse vividly described how the hospital greeted the news of the armistice: first with a shocked silence, then a pillow fight, and then a banquet and a ball.

'It was just the busiest time in the morning, dressings were in full swing, and the ward bore that look of importance which I always associated with it between the hours of 9am and 12pm,' she wrote. 'There's the dinner bell,' said Jumbo, a small person with an equally large appetite. 'Sure, man, you've only just had your breakfast,' said one of the Jocks. But right enough it was a bell and again and again it rang as if to repeat its message. Then someone in an incredulous voice said, 'Well boys, perhaps it's peace. The Armistice had to be signed before eleven o'clock this morning and perhaps they've signed it.' Perhaps, could it be – everyone was very quiet as if taking in the great possibility and awed by its magnitude. Then the definite news came. The ward echoed with the words, 'The war is over, the Armistice was signed at 5am'.

For a moment there was silence – 'an unusual commodity in a ward of British Tommies' – broken by laughter and a pillow fight that spared no one. Even the nurse who wrote about it fell 'victim to some four or five rounds of pillow ammunition'. Later that day, the Great Hall became the location for a celebratory banquet. Dinner was served to all 72 staff and patients, with 'Sister in charge of the punch bowl and flowers and smiles everywhere'. The main ward was turned into

an impromptu ballroom, the beds pushed to one side to make room for dancing, a few soldiers even dressing up as nurses (and fooling the village parson in the process). After four years of war, peace was celebrated at Dunham Massey with all due jubilance and glee.

With the war over, the auxiliary hospitals began to close. Lady Stamford admitted to her son that she hoped hers would shut soon. 'Things do not go very well now,' she wrote on 15 December 1918, 'and the staff all want to go away.'

By 24 January 1919, when the hospital finally closed, just one patient remained: Private Jenkins, whose septic foot left him so ill that Lady Stamford feared he might die. With heavy snow and the telephones down, she couldn't even contact the doctor for help. Jenkins somehow pulled through, and the last word must go to him, who on 2 February 1919 gave Lady Stamford his heartfelt thanks: 'I am writing this letter to you to express my gratitude for allowing me to remain in your house as I have got on exceedingly well since I have been here by myself … I am positively sure that if I hadn't come to Dunham Massey Hall when I did, I am afraid I should have only had one foot to walk on now. When I am able to walk about I should like to thank you personally for your kindness.'